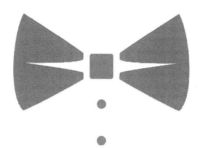

THE BEST MAN
project

DR. ABRAHAM SHANKLIN, JR.

Written By: Dr. Abraham Shanklin, Jr.
Produced By: Jabez Publishing House
Creative Designer: jMichael Advertising
Publishing Editor: Judi Light Hopson, Jabez Publishing House

DEDICATION

This book is gratefully dedicated to my sons Khoury, Jared, and Aldon, who continue to put a stamp on manhood in a powerful way, and whom I love more than words can ever express.

Also to the men who model true manhood for me; Dad Larry Titus, Paul James, Tyran Meredith, Keenan Meredith, Gerry Fernandes, and Glendon D. Jones.

To all of my spiritual sons but specifically, Wayne Turner Sr., Aaron Dada, Brandon Jefferson, Selton Shaw, Will Boone, and Kenny Williams, Jr., who are truly men after my own heart.

And finally to Ingrid, my beautiful wife, my first earthly love, whose faithfulness, patience, graciousness, support, and loyal love has been the foundation of my life and ministry. You are my encourager, my friend, my inspiration, my heart, my understanding, and my forever love.

WITH GRATITUDE

I want to say a special word of thanks to the New Life Fellowship family for their support and patience during the teaching of these Best Man Project messages. Your kindness, graciousness, and faithfulness help to give way to a message that I hope will become a movement and not just a moment.

Contents

FOREWORD

MY PAUL: A SPIRITUAL FATHER

Can you think of a book more needed than one describing and defining an authentic manhood?

Can you think of a man more qualified to write a book on authentic manhood than Dr. Abraham Shanklin Jr.?

The greatest problems in the world, with rare exceptions, all relate to men.

Crime	Drugs
Incarceration	Pornography
Spousal abuse	Desertion
Childhood abuse	Wars
Rape	Spiritual abuse
Violence	Sexual abuse

i

Need I continue? If the problems relate, by and large, to men, it is apparent the only answer for this global crisis is to address men head-on. But how? Through whom?

Dr. Abraham Shanklin Jr. is more than qualified to tackle this immense topic because of his military background, his years of pastoral ministry, his extensive discipleship training with men, his gifted abilities to exegete the Bible, God's Word, and the example of his life.

How can you become the best man for your wife, children, peers, church, community, and world? Dr. Shanklin lays it out in easy-to-understand, practical steps that eventually lead to liberty and transformation. More importantly, Abraham lives a life that gives him a right to say, "Follow me as I follow Christ." You can look at every part of his life. It's open and visible. He's vulnerable, and gives you the liberty to pursue growth through his example.

Millions of spiritual leaders invite you to hear them speak or preach, but rare is the leader who invites you to walk into his life and spend time with him. Because of your willingness to read this book, you've just opened the door to transformation and change. Congratulations!

But for this transformation to work, before you can

become the *best man*, it will require that you pass it on to other men. If you keep it to yourself, you will lose it; if you give it away, you will keep it. It's not enough to have one *best man*; we need a nation and world of them. Come on; let's start the ball rolling.

Larry Titus, President

Kingdom Global Ministries, Grapevine, TX

My Barnabas: A Spiritual Brother

S everal years ago, a friend of mine was talking with me on the phone and ended our dialogue with a curious question.

"Do you know Abraham Shanklin?"

"No, I don't," I responded.

My friend's response to me was immediate.

"You MUST connect with Abraham! He's just awesome! And he reminds me of you in some ways. I think that the two of you are supposed to be friends."

While I consider myself to be a friendly man, I must admit that I was not very keen on the idea of a 'cold call' in search of a new friend. Also, as a pastor whose 24-hour daily business is people, I wondered internally whether I had enough relational bandwidth to take on a new friend at that time. I decided to be polite and take down Abraham's contact information, while doing my best to conceal my lack of enthusiasm for the idea.

"Okay Larry. I'll be sure to reach out to him."

Now if I am being truly honest, and I am, my coolness to the idea of reaching out to this stranger all those years ago was not fully indicative of my preoccupation with the ministry. At the time of Larry's bold charge to me, I was a deeply wounded warrior in mourning. This was because during that period of my life, several of my colleagues had bitten the dust with regards to pastoral ministry. Some of these men of God were overtaken by a deep-seated discontent with their seemingly dull existence in the straight life, as pastors. Others of these men were experiencing acute mid-life crises, wherein they were questioning everything—including the relevance of their Christian faith, which was supposed to undergird their devotion in service to God and His people. Still others experienced moral failures in illicit relationships with women who were not their wives (sometimes their own parishioners). I had walked in accountability relationships with some of these men. And when their lives detonated, my connection with them as men and as colleagues often became a casualty of their life choices. I was probably a little gun-shy at the prospect of forming new friendships. I remained faithful in ministry, but I was also devastated and lonely. Maybe my wise friend sensed this in me. I now realize that despite the varied dilemmas that faced my fallen comrades, there was one common thread throughout all of their stories.

I wish I could say that I heeded my friend Larry all those years ago, and called Abraham Shanklin, who is the author of this book. I didn't. A few months went by and Abraham, instead, called me in response to a similar conversation about me that he had with our common friend. Some of the very best things God does in our lives have nothing to do with us at all. Life's best gifts are neither born from our merit nor our virtue. They are simply expressions of God's grace toward us. Abraham Shanklin is one of these 'grace gifts' in my life. You see, I needed Abraham to call me. This is because I had no idea how much I needed him in my life. Not long after our initial phone conversation, we decided to meet up at a restaurant at a central point between our two cities. We both sensed that God might be up to something in bringing us together. Neither of us knew the half of what God was doing. We discovered that we were both the same age, we were born in the same month of the same year, and that we had pioneered our churches within months of one another. We also realized that we had remarkably similar life pilgrimages, purpose, and perspectives. We discovered that we suffered similar pains, predicaments, and peccadillos. We even subsequently learned that we often preach the same subject matter from two different pulpits in two different states, repeatedly over the course of the year, without speaking to one another or comparing notes. It seems God has synced us—almost like one man in two bodies. Quite simply, Abraham Shanklin is my parallel companion. He is the man in my mirror. He is my spiritual doppelgänger. Just when I was feeling that I was fighting crime all alone in my native Gotham city, I discovered that there is a man with an 'S' on his chest 100 miles south of me doing the same in his own Metropolis.

The writer of this book is the chief factor that keeps the levee of my manhood strong and robust. I talk real talk with this man that goes far beneath the surface of typical male engagement. There is nothing that I feel I could NOT tell this man. Abraham has taught me to laugh at my storms rather than dread them. My demeanor is largely a byproduct of our monthly meetings over catfish, grits, and pancakes off a major Interstate (Real men eat good food!). During these encounters

I have had the distinct privilege of benefiting from my friend's finely honed listening skills. Every man needs to be heard, known, and understood. You will find within the pages of this book clear evidence that the author has listened to many men. You will also note a diagnostic brilliance in the author that addresses the challenges we face in a culture that is growing increasingly hostile toward men. You will further find this book to be not only profound in its content, but also practical in its solutions to real-life manly dilemmas. Abraham possesses a unique ability to communicate deep truths in a manner that resembles low-hanging fruit. We can all get something useful, if we just reach out a little bit from where we are.

This is not a book just for men. This is also a book for women who love men. Or at least women who love one man. This is not just a Christian book, although its author is a faithful follower of Jesus. This is a book for the faithful and irreligious alike. The state of manhood is in such dire straits that we have no time to quibble over the finer points of religious minutiae.

So pull up a chair at our table. Abraham and I have been waiting for you to join in on our dialogue. We just ordered some catfish, grits, and pancakes. But if you don't mind, I'm going to be silent from this point. My friend, the author, is more than capable of carrying the conversation from here.

The topic? Manhood.

The forecast? A storm is coming.

The dilemma? The levees are weak.

Read on.

Paul J. James, Founding Senior Pastor
Careview Community Church, Lansdowne, PA

FOREWORD

MY TIMOTHY: A SPIRITUAL SON

I met Dr. Abraham Shanklin Jr. in 2007 after visiting the church he pastors a few times, with my then girlfriend, and now wife. It wasn't long after I started attending Sunday services that we struck up a friendship that has grown into more than I could ever imagine, in a relational aspect. Bishop Shanklin sensed early on—through what could only be the Holy Spirit—that I needed much more than a traditional pastor/church member relationship.

What I needed was the spiritual guidance that Paul gave Timothy throughout the New Testament, showing him the true path of Christ in the Word and through his life. It was during a Christian men's conference that Dr. Shanklin truly opened up to me and invited me into his life as his spiritual son.

Under Dr. Shanklin's watchful care, he has not only birthed me in the ministry as a son, but he has shown me, through his life and through his blameless character, without arrogance or self-righteousness, how to thrive as a Christ-centered man, husband, and father. Whether it's opening up his home or his nearly thirty-plus years of experience in the ministry of serving Christ, Dr. Shanklin has never waned in pouring out his heart and wisdom to bring me closer to God.

This has included challenging me to press harder in the Word and dig deeper in the things of God, continually refining my character to conform to the image of Christ Jesus. It hasn't always been easy, being pressed to reach higher as Dr. Shanklin's spiritual son, but it has always been a blessing, as his iron sharpens my own.

When Dr. Shanklin told me he was putting this manuscript together on manhood, I thought of no one better to write such a book. With a resume that reads as a faithful husband for going on three decades, a dedicated father of four, and a bishop in the Lord's Church—who walks constantly with integrity and a reputation in the community as a leader of leaders—Dr. Abraham Shanklin Jr. has all the credentials *and more* to chronicle the steps to becoming a better man.

What's even more special about him is that he is a man willing to share from his vast wealth of knowledge in the Word of God and through his personal experience as a man of character. This book is a testament to that.

Selton Shaw, one of the spiritual sons

Laurel, MD

PROLOGUE

I wanted to begin with a poem I wrote back in 2007 and presented at a Man Up men's conference, where I had the privilege of speaking. It still rings fresh in my heart, as though I wrote it yesterday.

REAL MEN

I hurt for men, who pick up guns instead of picking up God,

I hurt for men, who pack lies instead of stacking truth,

I hurt for men without their little boys to raise, and little boys without their fathers,

I hurt for men, who hit their wives instead of helping their wives,

I hurt for men, who live like paupers, instead of like kings,

I hurt for men, who are running to death instead of running to destiny,

I hurt for men, who conceal their emotions instead of revealing their eternity,

I hurt for men, who have walked away from integrity and walked toward impurity,

I hurt for men, who don't see God visions and dream dreams,

I hurt for men, who don't know when to man up!

Real men praise their God and their wives,

Real men run toward their Goliaths, not away from them,

Real men pray,

Real men play,

Real men don't send their family to church; they bring them to church,

Real men make their yes a yes and their no a no,

Real men admit when they are wrong,

Real men love after their wives not lust after women,

Real men don't just drop a seed, but stay behind to help raise that seed,

Real men lead when they should lead, and follow when they should follow,

Real men can be and will be called A MAN!

I wrote that poem with a deep passion for encouraging men to be men. What was true then is true now; our identity as men has been taken and reworked because of a few bad apples. Now, I am not saying that there are not any real men, but they are being marginalized and underemphasized by a culture that seeks to reverse the years of wrong caused by men.

The Best Man Project was a vision I received 30,000 feet in the air while flying back from a West Coast men's event. The weekend was filled with incredible stories of men changed from the inside out. I have attended many men's conferences and taught at my share of them, but something clicked in me. I knew I wanted to do more; I needed to do more to help the men in my local church, my contact lists, my culture, and even my country with reclaiming their manhood and masculinity.

This book is for you if you feel like you are struggling with an identity crisis of masculinity. This book is for you if you have questions about the man in manhood. This book is more than just a message, but a movement out of neutral and back into your God-given role.

There is so much being said about men from every corner and sector of life. We are being inundated and overwhelmed by everyone seeking to redefine manhood into a new kind of normal—being a man without the masculinity. I say you can't have one without the other.

That's what this book is all about. It's about men repudiating the life without true masculinity and becoming real men of God. It's about men rediscovering manhood and walking in that discovery.

This book is about men learning how to be a man, see himself as a man, live in the freedom as a man and then channeling that into the best man, husband, father, and brother. It's about knowing your spiritual DNA, character, commitment, and influence despite past setbacks and present pressures. That's the kind of man I want to be. Will you be my *best man*?

It's my contention that when men know God and know themselves, they truly will be men! Welcome to *The Best Man Project*!

CHAPTER 1

Manufacturing A Character

Filling A Role

Do you remember the day you decided to get married? It was no doubt the most important day in your life, next to landing that dream job, the birth of your firstborn, or buying your new home. It would be the day you would announce to the whole world, "I am getting married!" So, the ring was bought, the questioned was asked ("Will you marry me?"), and the answer was yes. Now the next most important thing of all—who will you choose as your best man? Who will be the man who will stand next to you, not to throw you a wild bachelor party or to hold the ring, but the man who will cover you, defend you, or fight for you?

The best man is usually a term reserved for the highest-ranking groomsman in a wedding. Perhaps he is the one who has known the groom the longest, or the one whom the groom considers to be his best friend. In some instances, the best man may be the eldest brother of the groom; in other cases, he could be the male best friend of the bride. Whether one is offered this position because of family history or proven friendship, it is not something that is taken lightly. The best man plays a significant role, not only in the wedding, but also in the life of the groom.

The role of the best man is so important that Hollywood produced a movie entitled *The Wedding Ringer*, starring Kevin Hart, Josh Gad, and Kaley Cuoco. The film features a young man preparing to marry the love of his life, only he has no friends and therefore no one to select as his best man; so he hires Kevin Hart's character, who owns Best Man Inc., a company that provides attendants for friendless grooms. The emphasis of characters played in a wedding ceremony is so important that people trade true value in order to fill what they believe to be voids in their lives. This is not only true for weddings; it is also true for other areas of our lives. In this movie, Kevin Hart's character spends time getting to know the groom-to-be. He works to develop fictional storylines to convince the bride and family that they have a long-standing history, dating back to college, and they truly are best friends. When we look at this film, we find the role of the best man explored in a way we have never considered. It speaks to the importance of friendship, trust, and history that goes into making an important decision. While the film kept us laughing throughout, it also educated us on how we process and think of someone we consider a best man. How many of us have connected with men who did not display virtues and values worth emulating? Men of little value and even less character because we were trying to fill what we thought were voids in our lives? In the case of *The Wedding Ringer*, the groom-to-be actually spent thousands of dollars creating a character to play a role in his life. Is this not like so many of us, spending time, money, and resources with men we call brothers, or even best friends?

In the end (spoiler alert) Josh Gad's character discovered qualities in Kevin Hart's character that should be seen in every man, across the nation and around the world. Those characteristics that he discovered led both men to develop a genuine bromance. Josh Gad's character realized that he had a true man standing by his side, not just the hire-for-pay stand in. The qualities that both characters discovered didn't have to be manufactured, because they were qualities they already shared.

That is what I seek to unveil in the chapters ahead: the characteristics that you saw in your best man, or those same characteristics that were seen in you that led you to be selected as a best man. Talking it out is what I want to do. Throughout this book, I choose to be the enforcer of encouragement. You will not be emasculated, but emancipated, from the culture's image back to Christ's image.

Just because you know the name of the man doesn't mean you know the man.

AFTER THE MOVIE STOPS

If I were to line up a host of male celebrity actors, I'm sure many of us would raise our hand and say with all certainty that we know who they are. Dwayne "The Rock" Johnson, Anthony Hopkins, Al Pacino, Denzel Washington, Justin Timberlake, Idris Elba, T.D. Jakes, Kevin Hart, Leonardo DiCaprio, Morris Chestnut, Brad Pitt, Morgan Freeman, Steve Harvey, and Robert DeNiro are just a few of the leading actors that I'm sure most people would say they know very well. But I submit to you that just because we know the name of the man doesn't mean we know the man. Who is behind the role, looking through the lenses, or hiding behind the masks of hypocrisy? There is a difference between playing a character and living with character.

Men have been forced to play parts that they didn't ask for. If they show any type of strength, then they are being too aggressive. If they show no emotion, then they are too hard. Men have been reduced to merely what's below their belts, and given no credit for what's above their neck. Simply because you know what to call him doesn't mean you know what he is thinking, how he is feeling, or even where he is going.

NOT ABOUT A ROLE

We need to rediscover and reclaim our manhood. This journey is for men—brothers, fathers, and sons—and for the women who want to see men operating in their God-designed roles. This is about getting ahold of our proper bearings on this subject of manhood that has been skewed for a long time.

I don't know about you, but I am ready to move forward with some fresh perspective and renewed purpose. This book is not about playing the role of a man. It's about being a man unapologetically and unashamed; that's the man I want to be. Will you stand with me?

INTRODUCTION

MANUFACTURING CHARACTER - I submit to you that just because we know the name of the man doesn't mean we know the man. Who is behind the role, looking through the lenses, or dangling around the curtain? *There is a difference between playing a character and living with character.* Men have been forced to play parts that they didn't ask for.

DISCUSSION QUESTIONS

1. Think about the roles you have had to fulfill over the course of your life. Describe the easiness or difficulty of stepping into those roles. Did you have help?

2. Could you name some of the men who have served as role models for you? What would you say was the most valuable trait you picked up?

3. In this chapter, we read that the Best Man plays a significant role in the life of the groom. Name one of the ways your Best Man assisted you on your wedding day. If you are not married yet, what qualities would you be looking for in your Best Man?

4. What comes to your mind when you hear words like manhood and masculinity? How are your views different from those of your friends?

5. What is the one area in your life that needs an immediate adjustment? Are you ready to go from playing a role to being authentic?

MOVING FORWARD

Men have been often redefined and redesigned by the culture, but today you can take the step to move back toward being celebrated for who you really are. No more pretending and no more excuses. You are more than a donor.

CHANGING YOUR MIND

Then God said, "Let Us make man in Our image, according to Our likeness. – Genesis 1:26

A Man's Prayer

Lord, make me so mighty against the deadly undertow of self-defacement and purposelessness that I am never ashamed to trust your arm, like a child with his father, in every breaking wave. Amen!

CHAPTER 2

CAN I BE A MAN PLEASE?

GROOMING YOUNG MEN

God's original intent for us is that we be like Him. Made in His image and groomed in His likeness, we have the very character of God—a speaking spirit, living on the inside of us. The problem is that God can't be read, He must be revealed. As little boys, we grow up searching outside of ourselves for our identity, when the essence of who we are is buried like a treasure hidden in a field. Perhaps we grew up without a father in the home, as a product of divorce. Some of us grew up raised by the older guys in the neighborhood, or influenced by the characters we saw on television or music videos. For some, we watched our mothers being abused by our father, step-father, boyfriend, or pimp. There are those of us who were raised by a big brother, uncle, or grandfather, who may not have known themselves what true masculinity was. Whether we were born into a family with a gated fence, two dogs, and a nanny, or were abandoned by a drug-addicted parent who had no idea who he or she was, we have unknowingly modeled our lives after environmental factors—not the original intent of God's plan and purpose for our lives. It does not matter how we were born; we must all be born again! We are all one discovery away from knowing who we are as men.

Today, we sound the alarm on the crisis breaking out in our community where men are concerned. We live in a society in which masculinity is minimized whenever possible, and the idea of being a godly man is strongly condemned. As a pastor, my heart breaks when I see young boys struggle to find themselves, particularly those who are growing up in single-parent households, or being raised by grandmothers trying to keep the family together, due to unfortunate circumstances created by the parents. There are many factors involved in a young man's development that impact how he sees himself and how he sees the world around him. In a search to find himself, he looks for validation in other men, who may or may not know who they are. If there is no father in the home, the young man will find the next closest male to model himself after. In instances where there are fathers, step-fathers, or live-in boyfriends in the home, the young boy is also likely to either repeat the behavior he sees from the male in authority, or defy the odds by becoming a total opposite. Young boys need their fathers, but grown men need them even more.

I was speaking to my congregation and edifying the men to stand with me and give a voice to the silent killer: systematically desensitized manhood, converting us all into an effeminate community. In a rousing ovation of thunderous applause and high praise, the church erupted as men joined with me as a symbolic gesture of the restoration of manhood to God's original intent for the man, declaring from a 1960s pronouncement, "I am a man!" I looked over and noticed a young boy who was apparently uncomfortable in this environment, as he tucked his head beneath his grandmother's arms. She held on to him looking on at me as if I was an offense to her and her grandchild. I challenged some men to go and speak into that young boy's life. The grandmother seemed horrified that we would dare call out to the man inside the boy. She didn't understand that a woman, no matter how caring and endearing, could never help a boy transition to manhood.

She has no experience being a man, thinking like a man, or having had experiences like a man. To this day, she has not returned to the church and my heart breaks every time I think of the little boy and how keeping him from the influences of godly men may lead him to be conflicted and confused about his male identity. I have heard my share of moms calling their sons "baby boy," but don't understand that as he grows older and he looks in the mirror, a baby is not what stares back at him. How far we have fallen from the faith, as God's original intent and plan for mankind has become an offense even in the house of worship.

WHERE ARE THE MEN IN THE CHURCH?

A sacred and hallowed ground, the church has become a less-than-attractive place for men. I believe that it takes a man to raise a man. There are a lot of positive organizations and men's groups that can help bring to light the qualities of manhood and masculinity. The church has often not been the best beacon for manhood training and development.

In the church, the woman's dominant presence is bittersweet. It is the women who are literally keeping the doors of most churches open today. Most congregations are overwhelmingly filled with women. The role women play in ministry is critical, and that's why we must let them know how much we as men need them in this critical hour. But we all know that too much of a sweet thing is not good for us, and we need balance in our lives. The bitterness many men have with the church is that it has become too feminized. Men are often turned off by the feminization of the church. There are so many messages in the church for and about women. While women are flocking to conferences and buying books, men have very little to run to when it comes to manhood. As women are being loosed each year at major conferences and talking about being loosed, men are stuck between a rock and a hard place with no one giving a voice to the silent killer, the *broken place*. And this is particularly true in minority-led churches.

WHERE ARE THE MEN IN THE CULTURE?

Women are increasingly taking leading roles beyond the four walls of the church. Today, women are the leading demographic of subscribers on social media, and determining hot topics and trends impacting sales and generating revenue streams for businesses. Without question, women are gaining power, with their financial impact counting as 52% of the gross national product of

America. The voice of women is so strong that a candidate for presidency must go through their networks, which are set up to influence the times and change the seasons. In fact, there are more female candidates running for public office and being appointed to high-ranking positions in this country than ever before. This trend has emerged from the home dynamic of leading women, now to the point where we find the CEO of Yahoo making a bold statement when she defied the odds and returned to work almost immediately after having her baby. Women are no longer taking a back seat to men in the home, church, or in the marketplace. Whether you're watching *The Talk*, *The View*, or *The Chew*, women are redefining the flow of information and using the platforms in the marketplace to shape the minds of a captivated audience. Today, you can't turn on a network covering football and not find a woman either in the anchor chair, on the sidelines reporting updates, or providing commentary on game previews or the evening news. In fact, the NFL recently hired the first female referee to officiate games. While we celebrate the emergence of women trending in the world, there is a simultaneous pattern of men losing ground as the world and church both become a more effeminate place.

I am for women's rights but I am also for balance and sensibility. I believe there is room for men and women to operate freely in the church and in the marketplace, but we can't ignore the consequences brought on for men by the shift in dynamics. Smothered beneath the voice of the new trends is a pattern developing where men are increasingly finding it harder to find level footing. Who is giving a voice to the brother in need of guidance and direction? Where is the platform for men to work through or communicate the challenges we face, or the need to express ourselves constructively? How do we find a medium between what it means to lead and what it means to follow? We know that men are wired differently from women. Our sense of belonging comes differently. Invite us to a club, game or group, and we feel a part of and connected to something. We are brotherhood driven. For this reason, we gravitate to gangs when there is no balance in the home or a father look up to.

Young boys are constantly searching for role models because we think in patterns and structures.

Young boys are constantly searching for role models because we think in patterns and structures. Men pattern their lives after those who go before them. We seek out the best professional athletes and try to emulate them in what we do. We look at the older gentlemen playing horseshoes in the small park, and seek to have a beer with them and "kick the bobo." We search the room for the one who seems to be in authority, and try to make friends with him so we can gleam from his wisdom and learn how to lead. When the church is full of women, men tend to be drawn away. It is hard to compel a man to come to church, not because there are too many women, but because there are not enough men. It is my hope that *The Best Man Project* will help men break the silence on the epidemic and pandemic sweeping our nation and gaining momentum around the world. The masculine father figure was replaced by women who raised their boys toward manhood. This caused boys growing into men to believe that a woman's definition of a man was right. And any other idea of a man was wrong.

My wife came to grips with the reality of a man's influence in the lives of his sons. One day when our sons were younger, I got into an intense roughhousing match with them. I was working my hardest not to allow them to overtake me, and they were working their hardest to finally get their father to submit. Their mother, witnessing all of this, cried out, "Stop it, you are hurting them!" We immediately stopped what we were doing (and by the way, no one was broken up and no one was hurt.) I looked at her and gently reminded her that this is a rite of passage for young boys. This type of roughhousing between father and sons serves an evolutionary purpose, and actually provides a myriad of benefits for our progeny. The benefits far outweigh the apparent perceived visual battle scars and the cries of surrender. The benefits are that this interaction helps a young boy develop a resilient spirit, teaches him how to adapt quickly to unpredictable situations, gets him physically active, and he also develops a bond with his sparring partner, thus not being afraid of other males. It drives home how to manage pain and discomfort. That became a defining moment in our household, about allowing me, as their father, to shape their manhood and masculinity.

Now if we're going to fight the good fight for our sons, we need to learn our identity. Sons don't mind following someone who leads by example and leaves a trail right into the life of manhood. Are you up for the challenge?

It is hard to compel a man to come to church, not because there are too many women, but because there are not enough men.

REFLECTION PAGE

INTRODUCTION

CAN I BE A MAN PLEASE? - God's original intent for us is that we be like Him. Made in His image and groomed in His likeness, we have the very character of God – a speaking spirit, living on the inside of us. The problem is that God can't be read, He must be revealed. Today, we sound the alarm on the crisis breaking out in our community where men are concerned. We live in a society where masculinity is minimized whenever possible, and the idea of being a godly man is strongly condemned.

DISCUSSION QUESTIONS

1. When you were a little boy, what were some of your most memorable experiences that you learned from your father? If you grew up without a father, think about an encounter you had with a surrogate father.

2. Did you go to church growing up? Were there men in attendance? How would you describe the role they played in the church?

3. In this chapter, we asked the question, "Where are the men in the culture?" Do you agree with this section? Why or why not?

4. Do you feel greater pressure as a man and all that being a man encompasses, and how do you cope with the changing role of men in our culture?

5. What area in your life do you feel that you need to still need to grow in? How can the men around you help you in that?

MOVING FORWARD

Young boys are constantly searching for role models because we think in patterns and structures. It is time for us to take the opportunity grow up and go forward in our quest to redefine manhood in ourselves. Are you ready for the challenge?

CHANGING YOUR MIND

When in our rightful place as men, families are whole, marriages are productive and the marketplace is stable.

A Man's Prayer

Heavenly Father, Your majestic Name fills the earth! Thank You, Father, for men. Lord, I thank You for equipping me as a man to take my rightful place in You. Thank You for the men and boys who will join the body of Christ and glorify Your Name. Thank You, God, for restoration, reconciliation and healing that will come to men and young boys alike. Thank You, for giving us everything we need to live a godly life. Amen!

CHAPTER 3

ABSENCE

THE HEART OF THE MATTER

Before the foundation of the world, God made man in His image and likeness. Men are to be the expression of the God who created them. But the culture that we live in has worked to right the wrongs of men who have done their share of evil deeds against woman, child, and beast by redefining manhood. There is a push to turn the tide and declare the remaking of a new kind of man, minus the bravado: a new breed of man that is softer, a lot more passive, and greatly marginalized for a new millennium.

The heart of the matter is that all mankind is the creation

of God. As children of God, we not only bear the physical attributes given to us by our Heavenly Father, but we are defined by His decision to make a man distinctly different than a woman. Men were created to provide, protect, and secure their homes. This is not a competition with the opposite sex. We were created to be strong, courageous, brave, ambitious, and kingdom-minded. We thrive on taking territory, executing dominion, and expressing the authority we have been given in this world. As stated above in the previous chapter, when we as men are in our rightful place, families are whole, marriages are productive, and the marketplace is stable.

There is nothing worse than a man who is out of place.

When a man is out of position, the family is dysfunctional, marriage becomes obsolete, and the marketplace feels the impact. There is nothing worse than a man who is out of place. When men are not in their rightful place, they are desperately wicked and cannot be trusted. Because it is natural for man to *provide*, a confused man is stirred to defraud family, friends, governments, and even nations. A misplaced man whose nature is to *protect* will incite disputes, cause racial tension and divides, and even initiate wars. An untethered man whose nature is to *secure* will strike fear into his family, community, or nation to either deflect others' attention from his insecurity—due to not being in control, because he's not living in the expressed image of God with a king's dominion, or so that he can look like a savior—deceiving the public into terrorist threats only he can protect them from. However, the inherited nature of a man has amazing results when he's in his rightful place.

PANDEMIC

The state of manhood is seen in the crisis of manhood. No matter where you go in this world, you encounter man after man who is unsure about his role because he is unsure about who he is. Please understand me, this is not a lesson in skills, passions, and experiences. This is about what is at the core of every man—manhood. We have a pandemic on our hands when it comes to manhood and masculinity. America has a problem defining manhood. Africa has a problem defining manhood. Australia has a problem defining manhood. Every nation on the planet has a problem defining manhood. Just take a poll with any man on the street, asking him to define what he thinks manhood is. All of the answers are centered on what he *does* as a man, not who he *is* as a man. When I speak of a pandemic, I am addressing the widespread impact of men without a real clarity on who they are as men. There is nothing worse than a man with an identity crisis. A man who doesn't know who he is, is high risk. He has grown into the stature of a man, but he lacks the maturity of carrying out business and operating in his rightful place in this world. I see men in a state of confusion and facing challenges at every turn.

There is an absence of men standing up in the confidence of what they know are innate characteristics that set them apart from the opposite sex. Men are withdrawing from major institutions in our nation. They are rejecting institutions of higher learning and marriage. Men are opting out of traditional roles, because the roles have been rewritten.

A THEOLOGICAL REVELATION

I want to share with you a passage out of God's word that illustrates what happens when there is an absence of biblical manhood in our nation. In the Old Testament, we find a startling revelation nestled in the book of Isaiah Chapter 3. Look at verses 2–7 with me:

"He will take away all the heroes and soldiers. He will take away all the judges, the prophets, the fortunetellers, and the elders.

He will take away the army officers and important officials. He will take away the skilled counselors, the magicians, and those who try to tell the future.

He says, 'I will put young boys in charge of you. They will be your leaders.

The people will turn against each other. Young people will not respect those who are older. The common people will not respect important leaders.'

At that time a man will grab one of his brothers from his own family and tell him, 'You have a coat, so you will be our leader. You will be the leader over all these ruins.'

But the brother will refuse and say, 'I cannot help you. I don't have enough food or clothes for my own family. You will not make me your leader.'"

25

If you must, pause and reread the above verses again. Therein lies some of the most clear language reflecting the times we are living in. It is as if the prophet Isaiah was sitting at the courtside of our nation, calling the actions of this generation in which men who never grew up are in charge of governments, corporations, and communities. We have boys leading homes, and men who do not want to lead.

Let me say to the man who might be reading this book right now: we need you to make a comeback. We need you to reach deep within and say, "I will not remain absent." Repeat the words of the Apostle Paul in 1 Corinthians 13:11 over and over again:

"When I was a child, I talked like a child, I thought like a child, I reasoned like a child. When I became a man, I put the ways of childhood behind me."

REFLECTION PAGE

INTRODUCTION

ABSENCE - The state of manhood is seen in the crisis of manhood. No matter where you go in this world you encounter man after man who is unsure about his role because he is unsure about who he is. Please understand me, this is not a lesson in skills, passions, and experiences. This is about what is the core of every man – manhood.

DISCUSSION QUESTIONS

1. What thoughts come to your mind when you hear about a pandemic of manhood in our world? Could you describe your feelings on the matter?

2. Do you ever feel out of place as a man? What gives you hope in the midst of such an absence of strong manhood and masculinity?

3. In this chapter we read, "Our Heavenly Father made a man distinctly different than a woman." Have you ever felt in competition with women for acceptance and value in our culture? Why or why not?

4. Men were created to provide, protect, and secure their homes. Do you struggle with those responsibilities?

5. What is the one area in your life that you need to work on and work out as you seek to retreat or withdraw from actively engaging in redefining manhood and masculinity?

MOVING FORWARD

We were created to be strong, courageous, brave, ambitious, and kingdom minded. We thrive in taking territory, executing dominion, and expressing the authority we have been given in this world.

CHANGING YOUR MIND

When I was a child, I talked like a child, I thought like a child, I reasoned like a child. When I became a man, I put the ways of childhood behind me. – 1 Corinthians 13:11

A Man's Prayer

Lord, make me so mighty in resisting the bait of planned absenteeism, so that I am forever counted among the men who stand tall and proud. Help me not to withdraw from my family or my friends, but give me the strength to stay accountable. Amen!

CHAPTER 4

CHOOSING THE RIGHT MAN

If I were to ask you who you are as a man, could you articulate it without giving me your name, rank, and social security number? Don't give me your occupation, your job position, or any other titles people generally use to identify themselves. Could you simply tell me who you are? Not that your name and occupation don't matter; there are a lot of men who know their names and occupations, but don't really know the core of their being.

If God were to draw the picture of a real man, what would it look like to you? Would he be wearing a business suit and Italian loafers, driving a BMW 5 Series? Or, would he be tattooed up with a gold teeth grill, racing about town in a remodeled police cruiser with 24-inch spinning rims? Most of us better hope these types of images aren't the picture of a real man, because we should not be defined by what we wear or what we drive.

Is the right man somebody who goes around impregnating women? No, there are dogs that live their lives just to mate. Is the right man someone who beats women and struts around parading his superiority? Of course not—but who *is* he? We'd better move toward finding him *fast*, because our daughters are without access to men who have those godly qualities they are looking for.

MISIDENTIFICATION

We are making the mistake of defining men by their roles as husband, father, doctor, or plumber. By God's definition, a man is full, complete, integral; one in Him. When was the last time we celebrated a man for just being a man? Unfortunately, the world has compromised God's definition of manhood and replaced it with one of its own.

When was the last time we celebrated a man for just being a man?

When a man has not connected to true manhood and genuine masculinity, he could live a life full of selfish ambition, self-gratification, self-medication, self-indulgence, and self-worship. When a man goes from being selfless to being selfish, his immaturity breeds unbridled passions that are masked in his outward appearance. And there are those who mask their emptiness in power, believing that the more people and things they control, the better the chances they can control the things they never could before. A man who is not secure in bearing the image of our God is a man who is insecure in relationships, business deals, and ministry assignments. Yes, there are even broken men serving in the churches across our great nation. For women, the inherent danger of engaging a broken man is that women make the mistake of thinking they can say or do something to change him. Women often flock to men in church, because they assume that a man in church is a man in Christ. The risk one takes with entering into relations with a broken man is not only reckless but also dangerous. The savior mentality has resulted in so many failed marriages, ministries, businesses, and families. Only God can save a man. Only a man can want salvation for himself.

Another matter that causes the misidentification of a man is when he doesn't have a purpose for *why* he is doing what he does, which is directly tied to *who he is.* Many men only have the daily grind and routines of life. They get up in the morning to slog through the day, and trudge home every night with little or no sense of why they're doing what they do.

Since thinking about who he is, and what his purpose in life is, can raise some uncomfortable questions, a lot of men retreat to man caves, hide behind work, or live out their fantasies through other self-medicating means. These things may not be enjoyable, but they do provide a refuge.

Men have been misidentified in the last few decades, resulting in the producing of different models of men. It's as if a lab experiment produced a Dr. Jekyll and a Mr. Hyde. Which one will you choose: the distorted, disfigured, sub-human being seeking to become a menace to society or the brilliant, level-headed humanitarian, working to improve the society he lives in? You choose the right man.

THE HEART OF A MAN

As we move toward presenting the qualities that would redefine manhood and masculinity, allow me to talk about the genuine heart of a man. This indeed has to be connected to manhood. When under pressure or placed beneath a microscope, the heart of a man of God emerges with perseverance, endurance, and stamina. The will of a champion is birthed from a man who's spent time in the Word of God and has been changed by the renewing of his mind. When a man is one with God, he is patient, secure, confident, and wise. The issues of a man of God are not a matter of *if* he will be faced with hard trials and tribulations, but *how he draws strength* through the adversity. Instead of looking at the world around him and conforming to it, he is brave and courageously presses toward the mark of a higher calling.

The heart of man shaped and molded by God puts him squarely into the grooves of manhood and masculinity. It is like having rails which facilitate an easy train ride, moving about a certain area. If one rail is manhood and the second rail is masculinity, then the train is the man himself, easily moving about the journey of his life. As it was in *The Wizard of Oz*, the man does not have to go see the Wizard to get a heart as the Tin Man thought. He only needs to recognize that God has already made it new through Jesus Christ.

REALIGNMENT

Today, men need to be aware of the main ingredient in the heart that makes him a man after God's own heart—love.

The Apostle Paul wrote something very interesting in the context of marriage about this one characteristic that helps a man connect with his wife. It is one of the best ways for a man to align himself with the person of Christ. In Ephesians 5:25 he writes:

"Husbands, love your wives, just as Christ loved the church..."

He wasn't addressing merely an emotion here, as I can sense some of you who are reading this are squirming now, but this is an *action word*. This is the word that helps us to relate to our wives with love and sensitivity, while providing the godly leadership we're responsible to provide. I will discuss further in detail the husband-wife relationship in the chapter titled "The Best Husband."

But the reading in Ephesians records something else worth highlighting; if we can realign ourselves with it, we are steps closer to reclaiming God-designed, God-ordained manhood. Paul writes:

"In this same way, husbands ought to love their wives as their own bodies. He who loves his wife loves himself.

After all, no one ever hated their own body, but they feed and care for their body, just as Christ does the church— for we are members of his body." —Ephesians 5:28–30

Look at how poetic that sounds. A man can't really love his wife if he doesn't first love himself. How can you love someone you don't know? Many men don't know who they are, so self-love is hard, which is transferred to his God, his wife, his family, and his community. This type of man doesn't get any love because he hasn't been able to love himself. No excuse, just a reality.

But Jesus would invite us back to our first love (Revelations 2:4–5). Learning how to love Jesus helps us in learning how to love ourselves, which in turns helps us to love our wives, love our families, love our neighbors, love our church, and yes, even love our enemies from the heart.

I was struck with a powerful personal lesson about what it meant to love my wife by loving myself. Years ago, I had suffered a heart attack. It was due to a combination of genetics and poor eating habits. I wasn't really taking care of myself, and with the added stress from building a new church; it was not a good mix.

When she would remind me about my eating habits, I would immediately become defensive. I felt like she was nagging, and that really irritated me to no end. What I would eventually come to understand was that because I was not taking care of myself, I hated my own body—which led me to reject her concern for me. I didn't love *me* enough to watch what I ate and have regular checkups. To her, it meant that I didn't care enough about her feelings, and whether or not my actions could lead to her being a widow and leaving my children fatherless. As I write, I can feel the guilt over my foolish pride and how it could have devastated my family. When I learned to love myself, it taught me how to love her.

Men, love is at the core of what we were meant to be as men. It is a defining moment in our quest to redefine our manhood. It is not less than masculine to love, because it's not what I feel, *it is what I do.*

So, it's time to make a choice. No one will choose the right man until the right man comes along. You are the right man because God made you that way. I don't care what you have done in your past, you are still a man. I don't know what road you have decided to take, but you are still a man.

I am not certain what your future holds, but I do know that the man you are must take the lead.

Often we don't realize the impact our decision to grow has on others. While we once thought only little boys need a man to groom them, we now know that grown men need other men, too. Someone has to stand up and speak into the heart of men. There has to be a voice of a champion who has our permission to tell us who we are, and show us the *right path to take* so that we can stand proudly as men. Though flawed, men are able to navigate between strength and compassion, and our families can be healed, delivered, and set free. I believe King David is one man who is well able to do that for us.

Reflection Page

INTRODUCTION

CHOOSING THE RIGHT MAN - The heart of man, shaped and molded by God, puts him squarely into the groves of manhood and masculinity. It is like having two rails in which to facilitate a train to easily ride upon to move about a certain area. If one rail is manhood and the second rail is masculinity, then the train is man himself easily moving about the journey of his life.

DISCUSSION QUESTIONS

1. If you were handed a pencil and piece of paper and were asked to draw the image of a man, what are some of the items you would include in your drawing?

2. Are you comfortable with addressing the question about what your purpose in life is? What words would you use to describe yourself?

3. In this chapter it was stated that, "A man can't really love his wife if he doesn't first love himself. How can you love someone you don't know? Many men don't know who they are, so self-love is hard, which is transferred to his God, his wife, his family, and his community." Do you agree with this statement?

4. How actively involved are you in taking care of yourself? Do you have regular medical checkups? Would you say that it is easy for you to love as *an action*?

5. If you were to be given a heart condition test (i.e. emotions), what would be the rating you'd give yourself?

MOVING FORWARD

So, it's time to make a choice. No one will choose the right man until the right man comes along. You are the right man because God made you that way. It doesn't matter what you have done in your past, you are still a man.

CHANGING YOUR MIND

Men, love is at the core of what we were meant to be as men. It is a defining moment in our quest to redefine our manhood.

A Man's Prayer

Lord, make me so mightily unyielding to the enticements of selfishness that from my heart love forever flows. Help me to know who I am and give me the wisdom to communicate that. I want to be that man with the voice of champion for my generation. Amen!

CHAPTER 5

BE A MAN

In a lonely countryside, there was a young man faithfully tending to his father's sheep. He fearlessly defended them, with an eye toward completely fulfilling his responsibilities. That faithfulness was to be tested one day when dangers that confronted him tried to take what belonged to his father. In his own words he said:

> *"Your servant has been keeping his father's sheep. When a lion or a bear came and carried off a sheep from the flock,*

I went after it, struck it and rescued the sheep from its mouth. When it turned on me, I seized it by its hair, struck it and killed it.

Your servant has killed both the lion and the bear..."—1 Samuel 17:34–36

This same young man took on a Goliath and defeated him with just a slingshot and a stone. He would later endure being overlooked by his father as a potential successor to the throne of his nation. His life was filled with death threats, isolation, disrespect, jealousy, and even living as a fugitive from King Saul. Who is this man who displays such perseverance, tenacity, heart, and fortitude? Who is this man that defies the odds and becomes Israel's most beloved king? David.

THE KING WITHIN

There is a king inside of all men and a strong desire to express this kingdom on the earth as it is in heaven. When we don't know who we are, we have a distorted view of the qualities that God built into us. A perverted nature can and will cause us to misrepresent and misuse the power, ambition, drive, self-determination, conquering spirit, and other significant traits given to us by God. But here we have someone who can give us an up-close, objective lesson of manhood.

David was a man's man. We learn from his example because David's life is multifaceted. He was the ultimate alpha male, and he never stopped short of fulfilling his purpose during his time on earth.

BREEDING GROUND

Imagine the time when David is tending to the flock. There is no animal control or zoo to house the wild animals. At any given moment David could be faced with a menacing bear, tenacious lion, or a predatory fox. Whatever the challenge, David faced it head on and conquered them all. It was during this time that David penned the now famous Biblical verses we know as the book of Psalms. They are filled with the life lessons that brought to the surface the man he was.

While men rejected him, God called him king. How many of us have been the black sheep of the family, disowned by family and friends, or turned away because we didn't have "the look" or possess the strength to overcome? How many of us have watched other men seem to thrive and prosper, while we were forced to do the hard work in the field and not enjoy the fruit of our labor? Perhaps you are reading this book and you are a man who has been abused or neglected, and you feel that nothing good will ever come of your life. Now, David is reminding us all that it doesn't matter about your past, because God is a redeemer of pasts.

Some time ago, I was out cleaning my yard and noticed some old junk that ended up in the back near my property. It had been there for a long time, so I finally decided to move it. When I went to pick it up, there were all kinds of critters that had made their home under it and they began to move quickly to find a new home.

That incident reminds me that no matter what, like David, we need to pick up our lives—no matter what is hiding under them. No matter what is revealed, we need to move forward. We men have become very adept at covering things up. One of the things that causes us great pain is not knowing who we are and what we are supposed to do. For many of us, no one has pulled us aside and ushered us in. We had to pick it up on our own. I am not making light of anything you have gone through as a man, I'm just saying we all have a past that we need to deal with. David shows us life.

DISCOVERING THE TREASURE INSIDE

When David came out of the fields, the oil of God began to flow over him and he was anointed to be the next king of Israel. David had king in his blood, but his own father did not recognize it. And on top of that Samuel missed it too. Man looks at outward appearances while God looks at the heart—that is how Samuel would learn about God's selection process.

I believe as you are reading this book, you are beginning to feel for the first time in your life that you are accepted, valued, and loved. That you are not crazy about what you sense—that you are a man.

Some of us may have misinterpreted the circumstances into which we were born to mean there is no hope for us. Instead of being a product of our environment, we should have changed our environment by discovering the hidden treasure buried inside of us by the love of God.

On his way to being king, David used the tools he developed in the secret place of isolation to give him the courage to face a giant. So many men are experiencing emasculation by people who don't realize that there are certain characteristics critical for a man's development. It was the wilderness (root word: *wild*) experience that gave David the courage to face the giant, Goliath.

Facing the bears, lions, and God-only-knows what else is what prepared David for one of the biggest fights of his life. His triumphant victory over the giant Goliath became the signature of his legacy, as he made much with little—taking the giant down with a single flick of the wrist.

The soundtrack of his legacy would be sung throughout the regions; the man, with all of his highs and lows, would be remembered forever.

PASSING THE MANTLE

There are a myriad of books that have been written about this man's life. All of his life has been dissected and laid open for generations to read, revere, and stand in awe of his incredible life. There are moments, monuments, and movies about this well-lived life.

But there is one part of his life that captured my attention, and I just couldn't let it go. It was a moment when the man was old and near death (I am not celebrating his death, mind you). It was part of what would be his last words.

"So be strong and be a man."

Solomon, the son of Bathsheba, was the expected and crowned successor to his father's throne. I am certain that he had heard many words of wisdom from this beloved leader of Israel. David's final words to his son caught me off guard when I first read them, because I didn't expect them. I was riveted as I rehearsed them as though they were spoken to me.

This is what he said to his son:

"Now the time of David's death came near; and he gave orders to Solomon his son, saying, I am going the way of all the earth: so be strong and be a man."—1 Kings 2:1–2 (BBE)

A powerful statement, nestled right in the middle of a litany of final instructions. Of all the things that David could have said to his son, "be a man" has to be the most important thing he could have said to him. He didn't say be a king or be a leader...no, it was "be a man." This was indeed a passing of the mantle.

MEN NEED TO BE MEN

One man escorting another man to his rightful place into manhood; what men need to hear today is a voice saying to them, "Be a man."

Men need to be men because trials, defeats, and circumstances do not define you. Men need to be men because we don't trade our families for careers. Men need to be men because we don't sire children and then not stay around to raise them.

Men need to be men demonstrating servant leadership and liberating women from bad male leadership. Men need to be men who do not love power and money more than their wives. Men need to be men taking the lead in charity, church attendance, and cultural influencing.

Gentlemen, with that I am going to say to every man reading this book...BE A MAN!

REFLECTION PAGE

INTRODUCTION

BE A MAN - One of the things that cause us great pain is not knowing who we are and what we are supposed to do. For many of us, no one has pulled us aside and ushered us in. We had to pick it up on our own. I am not making light of anything you have gone through as a man, just that we all have a past that we needed to deal with.

DISCUSSION QUESTIONS

1. Have you ever been overlooked or passed up for a promotion? How did you react and what actions did you take?

2. When facing challenges in our lives, oftentimes we either run away or face up to them. Do you agree with that statement? Why or why not?

3. In this chapter it was written, "Of all the things that David could have said to his son, "be a man" has to be the most important thing he could have said to him. He wouldn't say be a king or be a leader...no, it was "be a man". Have you ever been told to be a man? If so, what were the circumstances surrounding the charge?

4. Have you ever read about the life of David? What inspires you the most about him and what he accomplished?

5. What areas of your life could you use David's life as example to step up? What examples of his life are you willing to pass along to another man?

MOVING FORWARD

King David of Israel is about to die and he's giving his final blessings on his children. He tells his son Solomon to, "Be strong and show yourself a man." There are very few times in the Bible when the word **man** means the characteristics of a man, the nobility of a man, the good things a man ought to be doing, and is not just referring to males. That's one of them.

CHANGING YOUR MIND

I am about to go the way of all the earth. Be strong, and show yourself a man. – I Kings 2:2ESV

A Man's Prayer

Lord, give me the wisdom to know who I am and what my God-given purpose is. You have made it clear that the steps of a good man are ordered by You. Help me to walk in those steps and follow a path of courage and confidence. I desire plans to pick up my life and keep on going no matter where I may have stumbled. With Your presence, I know that I can stand strong. Amen!

CHAPTER 6

I AM A MAN

One of the slogans that would strike down legalized segregation in the 1960s was "I <u>AM</u> a man." It challenged the centuries of dehumanization that had justified both slavery and Jim Crow. The verb in that slogan was capitalized and underlined for emphasis on signs used by marchers to symbolize a desire for better wages, better conditions, and a sense of dignity.

For generations, the ability to access violence has been one of the primary ways we defined manhood. From John Wayne to Clint Eastwood to Bruce Willis, the iconic man, the one boys were taught to celebrate and emulate, was the one who was good with his fists. But is that what manhood is all about? Is it who can deliver the greatest punch, or who has the greatest amount of possessions, or who can get the prettiest girl?

There are a number of great men I am thinking of who are doing the work to help us redefine our manhood and masculinity. Some are widely known, and others hardly known; yet their impact is no less helping to keep up the fight, across the nation and around the world.

Now is not the time to run, hide, or check out of this fight in our own local areas of influence. You can take what you have learned from the good men, rehearse it, and reinforce it in your own life, your son's life, and in your brothers' lives. Who knows? Maybe you were raised for such a time as this.

ORIGINAL INTENT

The original intent of God for man is that we function in this world bearing his image. It has never been the plan of God for us to become marginalized by the behavior of men behaving badly, and seeking to correct those ills with psychological strategic plans and experimental labs. We are mighty men of valor, not exhibits to be explored for testing.

Instead, we should be purposeful, deliberate, and intentional about our time on earth. It is vitally important that we understand that the attack on the family starts with the man. If the man is out of balance, the whole family becomes imbalanced. I reiterate what I have stated in an earlier chapter; this is not about competition with women for world domination. Nor can we right the wrongs of poor male leadership by trying to feminize males, attempting to remove or redefine masculinity.

As my friend and brother Paul James would say, "Men need to heal and women need to hope." I do not believe that healing will be found in a pill bottle as advertised in the latest late night infomercials or in a recent edition of an airbrushed men's magazine. Without question, work needs to continue in order to encourage strong men to step up to the plate and lead the way toward male wholeness.

WHICH MAN ARE YOU?

The subject of social dynamics is always an interesting matter of pursuit. The ability to know who you are is so paramount to restoring integrity and definition to the manhood crisis. Much work has been done to help further define the male in our culture. Aside from the God-given spiritual DNA of wildness, adventure, and danger to accomplish our earthly assignments of ruling, subduing, and dominating, I will take the time to further spell out the diversity that exists among men. All are needed in some way for balance and accountability. No one is any more or less valuable to the team called the MANHOOD roster.

ALPHA MALE

The alpha male is confident and believes he's clothed in immense power. He is sure of himself and has a very charismatic personality, which instantly draws people to him or repels them away from him. It's easy for the alpha man to engage socially, and he's easy to talk to. He's the type of man who doesn't make a big deal about leadership, because he's a natural born leader. As a little boy, he's the one who decides what all of his friends are going to do, dishes out assignments, and usually makes up the rules to the game. He's fearless and immortal, and he doesn't have a preference for seating or being placed in the front. As a natural born leader, his gift rises no matter where he's placed. His confidence can be misinterpreted as arrogance only because he is decisive and clear. Young boys with this type of personality who don't have the right guidance grow up to be controlling and stubborn. When guided, the alpha man gravitates to places of leadership and tends to be the strongest personality in the room; his presence is undeniable.

BETA MALE

Unlike the alpha male, the beta male is introverted in nature. He's shy and unassuming. He's a natural born follower and is not comfortable leading. He doesn't seek attention, and prefers to stay under the radar. He's the kind of person you can call whenever you need him, and he'll be there. The beta male has a very low profile, but is often the wisest among his friends. As a student by nature, he takes things in and takes his time processing them. He is slow to speak and quick to listen. He can be seen as non-aggressive because of his inherited nature, the impulse to be kind and extend grace to others. One of the greatest attributes of the beta male is that he is likely to stay loyal to you, even when you're wrong. He doesn't go with the crowd. In fact, he prefers handling business in the most discreet way possible. He is emotional, but from a distance. As a little boy, this personality type can be seen as soft by overly-aggressive male personalities. As one who is not known to be vocal or authoritative, he can assume the worst about himself and develop feelings of inadequacy, as if he is less than a man. Without proper guidance, he can drift off to be by himself too often, and alone with his thoughts. This is why it is important for a father to be present, so that he can properly discern the character of the beta male in his son, and provide his son's unique style of needed grooming accordingly. When under the right direction, the beta male personality is a strong tower and loyal friend. He is the kind of male who prefers to work behind the scenes without recognition in his family, ministry, and the workplace.

GAMMA MALE

Similar to the beta male is the gamma male personality, which stays under the radar as more of a strategic move than something he naturally gravitates to. He doesn't choose sides, and doesn't want to upset the rhythm of a thing. He intentionally hides himself behind the crowd and attempts to blend in. He's the kind of man who is likely to switch up depending on who is winning, or leans toward the majority. There is seemingly nothing spectacular about him, and he prefers to be more of an invisible guy. As a little boy, he is seen as a loner, or one who prefers a quiet place off in a corner. Other kids are likely to pick on him because they interpret his unassuming nature as detached and uninterested. Many boys with this personality fail to find their voice as young men and become passive-aggressive in their leadership. They are the kind of people that are frustrating for others—who come to expect him to give what he doesn't have, when he's occupying a role or position. For instance, he may be incapable of making a decision without running it by people he trusts. He is more of a token leader than one who can function independently of someone else's opinion.

SIGMA MALE

The sigma male is the wild card. He is the most difficult one of the four male traits to identify. He is intuitively cunning and savvy. If he's talking faster than you can listen, you're probably being manipulated. He's neither a leader nor follower, which makes him hard to figure out. In fact, he is more powerful than the alpha male in public, because he is so compelling and persuasive. He's the man who can sell water to a drowning man. As a little boy, he's the trickster and instigator. This personality is the one who can convince time to slow up to accommodate his need for just a few more seconds to get his point across. This young man is a jack-of-all-trades, and tends to enjoy learning new things so that he can engage people of all types, ages, and backgrounds. Expect the unexpected from the wild card. Just when you thought you had him figured out, know that you are only just beginning. He's the type of person who changes the rules as the game goes along.

This list of male personality types is by no means

exhaustive or exclusive. I believe that there is a little bit of each in all of us, but you know where you most often gravitate. Whether you are an alpha, beta, gamma, or sigma, there is no denying that you are a man.

A THOUGHT FOR CONSIDERATION

Being a man has nothing to do with one's age or physical stature. As we learned with David's appointment as king, God doesn't look on the outward appearance. Instead, He's looking inside the heart of a man to see a mirror image of Himself.

We've spent enough time in the laboratory of the culture, and allowed its systems to hold its exhibitions and experiments with us long enough. Let us see ourselves as God sees us. Let us speak of ourselves as God speaks of us. Let us act in a way that God would act. By doing so, we denounce the definition of the world's agenda to emasculate the male, and we breed a fresh perspective of God-designed and ordained masculinity.

There are many areas a male must operate in for God to see Himself in him. We are going to continue to explore and embrace them, in hopes of opening our eyes to a brand new day.

"We've spent enough time in the laboratory of the culture."

DESIGNED FOR DOMINION

Accepting life on its own terms means we don't complain when life gives us challenges. A real man knows that he is not operating off of his own ability, but God's ability. As a result, he believes no matter what happens or doesn't happen, he sees the world through the eyes of God and is confident he will find his way back to what he was always meant to be.

Have you ever purchased an electronic device and enjoyed exploring all of the exciting features, until you saw someone else with the same device doing far more with it than you? Either you didn't read the manual and learn all of the hidden treasures buried in the coding of the device, or you didn't realize you could refresh your device with instant downloads and experience all the excitement of the person right next to you.

As men, how many of us have unwisely compared ourselves to other men who appeared to be doing far more than we were? Or, have learned that the man next to us, who obviously has the same 24 hours a day and 7 days a week we are allotted, was experiencing different results?

Today, God is calling all of us back to the manual. Looking away from the creation and to the Creator, I believe there is no better place to discover the full expression of God's image and likeness than the Word of God. The manual is explicitly clear that we are born in the image and likeness of our God. To this end, we know there is some untapped potential and unused data waiting to be discovered. We were made to do something, say something, and be something! We were made to rule, subdue, and dominate!

Say it with me, "I AM A MAN!" And when you see yourself as a man, it helps you to better view how that is demonstrative in your role as a husband, father, and brother. I hope that the next few chapters make that clear for you. Read on...

REFLECTION PAGE

INTRODUCTION

I AM A MAN - The original intent of God for man is that we function in this world bearing his image. It has never been the plan of God for us to become marginalized by the behavior of men behaving badly and seeking to correct those ills with psychological strategic plans and experimental labs. Being a man has nothing to do with one's age or physical statue. As we learned with David's appointment as king in the last chapter, God doesn't look on the outward appearance to make his choice.

DISCUSSION QUESTIONS

1. How would you define manhood? Have you often described it in terms of what you do as a man rather than who you are?

2. Have you ever compared yourself to other men? Did it help give you greater direction, or did it discourage you because you didn't measure up?

3. In this chapter, several types of males were defined? Which one are you? Think about how that influences your family and other relationships.

4. You were designed for dominion. What are some of the images that come to your mind when you hear that statement?

5. What is the one area that you need to improve upon when it comes to knowing who you are? Are you able to say with confidence that you are a man?

MOVING FORWARD

Say it with me, "I AM A MAN! And when you see yourself as a man, it helps you to better view how that is demonstrative in your role as a husband, father, and brother.

CHANGING YOUR MIND

Let us see ourselves as God sees us. Let us speak of ourselves as God speaks of us.

A Man's Prayer

Lord, make me so mighty in seeing and mighty in savoring the promises of your sovereign grace that in all my sorrows I might never cease to be what you have called me to be. Thank you for helping me to understand that being a man has nothing to do with one's age or physical stature. Help me to know that whether I am an alpha, beta, gamma, or sigma man, I am still a valuable part of the human race. Amen!

CHAPTER 7

THE BEST MAN

Why *The Best Man Project?* I wanted to reignite for some, and reinforce for others, those qualities that define the manhood and masculinity that exist in every man. It was the qualities you saw in your best man that you didn't know also existed in you. You couldn't articulate why he was your partner, your ride or die. *What was it?...* you're thinking. You see a lot of yourself in him...his courage, his encouragement, his confidence, his vision, or his passion. You can't exactly put your finger on it, but you know, somehow you sense it—that's a real man.

Let me lay out for you those characteristics of a man that can't be denied. Embrace them and experience the exilaration of masculinity the way God intended. Reject them and continue to be tossed in a perpetual state of confusion and conflict. I don't want that. How about you?

MANHOOD 101: YOU ARE WILD

Have you ever wondered why Adam was created in a wilderness and Eve created in a garden? Have you ever stopped to considered why God used words like rule, subdue, and dominate? It may very well point to the fact that God outfitted him with a wild side.

There was a study conducted to demonstrate the inherited differences between a boy and girl. Two little girls were left in a room alone and after a while, the conversations started; the girls began to talk about their day and how they were feeling about different things. When two boys were left in a room alone, the results were quite different. When the conversations started, one boy tried to convince the other that he could beat him climbing to the top of the file cabinet. This demonstration speaks to the nature of the origin of each. While women have a natural gravitation to the expression of emotion, men tend to lean toward the more recreational and adventurous side of their being. A boy has a natural desire to explore the world around him. Boys enjoy the danger associated with activities that bring out the wild side of them.

Don't confuse being wild with unbridled bad behavior, or crimes committed against humanity. This is not a license to condone or support actions by evil men who seek to promote evil deeds. But John Eldridge, the author of Wild at Heart, defines this wild this way: "Man was born from the Outback, from the untamed part of creation."

You couldn't help it when you were a little boy; you wanted to climb a tree, throw a rock, play in the dirt, jump off the top step, run as fast as you could, or take apart that truck. You can't help it now that you are man; you want to drive fast, roller coasters give you a rush, owning a motorcycle appeals to you, hunting, hiking, and hitting the links stirs you up.

You want to be wild, but the world misinterprets this wildness as boyish immaturity or a display of man-boy antics from someone who won't grow up.

Don't they know the wild in you is how you tackle the wildernesses of your life? Yes, you are a responsible man who goes to work and contributes productively to society. You provide for your family, and serve your church and community. The debt you create is paid without a complaint and your taxes are serviced on time.

But you know that you were created for more than the regular mundane responsibilities of the day. Who you are and your purpose supersede a paycheck and a time clock. If the wild in you is not allowed to be expressed, then you are reduced to nothing more than a domesticated animal on display in a zoo.

When an animal is taken from the wild and caged, he loses his competitiveness, his alertness, and his ability to stay engaged with his surroundings. There is no fight left in him, and his capacity to face challenges becomes dull.

God made you with a wild side for a reason, and it is now time to reignite it. Shake the cobwebs off that wild nature and do something exciting again. Deny what you already know no longer—man, you are wild!

Have you ever noticed the process of a caterpillar transitioning into a butterfly? Consider the way it buries itself in the cocoon until it is ready to break through. How thoughtful of us to make the transition easier for the caterpillar by slicing the cocoon open so the butterfly can be released. However, that is not what God had in mind. The butterfly actually needs to break through the cocoon on its own, and emerge into the world in full bloom. Interrupting the natural process of the butterfly can cause it to miscarry its natural ability to draw enough strength from the secret place to allow it to soar in its full term.

How many of us have had mothers, sisters, grandmothers, and wives try to make our transition into manhood easier by stopping us from falling, preventing us from participating in controlled contact sports, or silencing our need for recreational companionship?

Is it possible that had David not been allowed to explore this wild side as a boy, he would not have had the strength to slay Goliath or lead a nation in battle? How much further along would some of us be, if we were not robbed of the opportunity to live out our wild side?

MANHOOD 102: YOU ARE ADVENTUROUS

Winston Churchill, now he was a man's man. Winston Churchill was an inspirational statesman, writer, orator, and leader who led Britain to victory in the Second World War.

"All his life," William Manchester writes, "Churchill loved to look at maps, as much for their utility as for their ability to stoke his imagination. Maps and naval charts lifted him away to far-off places and conjured images of heroic adventures long past." Churchill saw his entire life as a romantic adventure—a hero's journey.

Did you know that you are designed for adventure? God has given you the gifts of excitement and challenge. Think about all those activities that caused you to take the risks that changed your life. Some of your most successful accomplishments came because you accepted the challenges head on. Yet even your failures or missteps didn't tame you, because they inspired you to go out and try again.

That sense of adventure is why men fly planes, bungee jump off bridges, climb Mt. Everest, ski down mountain slopes, or scuba dive in the ocean depths. This appetite for excitement is what men live for, and some will even die for.

I am not asking you to go tomorrow and sign up for parachute lessons, but you must find ways to reignite the adventure in your everyday life. You were made for more than the mundane, but action, competition, and just good old rivalry that might be lacking in your life. Men don't go looking for a fight, but we don't run from one either.

Even if you are not a man who enjoys everyday physical activity or exploring adventures through digital platforms, you cannot deny that you were not meant to hibernate in some isolated space in your home, alone and without life. Perhaps you are a Renaissance man, entrepreneur, actor, soldier, or political activist. One thing we cannot deny is wherever we find ourselves, we will not take things lying down.

WHAT IS ADVENTURE?

Let's just outline a few of the essential elements of what will make your adventure an experience you embrace rather than reject.

Don't be afraid to fail. An adventure must have an element of risk: a chance that you may fail in the endeavor and/or become injured in some way. The most potent adventures carry the risk of physical harm or death, but financial, social, and emotional challenges can feel like adventures as well.

You don't have to be in control all the time. If you know exactly how an endeavor will start, proceed, and end, it isn't an adventure. An adventure must have an element of the unpredictable and unexpected.

Challenge yourself. An adventure can't be completely easy, and must at times call upon your ability to dig into your deeper qualities and skills. Two of the most fundamental traits activated by a true adventure are resolution and courage, which are necessary to propel you onward when the endeavor becomes scary and/or difficult.

You were made for adventure. That is who you are, and what you are made of. No one can take it from you, because it is a part of your DNA. So what are you waiting for? Put this book down for now, and go do something exciting!

MANHOOD 103: YOU ARE DANGEROUS

You are dangerous, period. I am not talking about the kind of danger that causes people to be afraid of you, and thus causes them to seek out ways to bridle your inherent manhood and masculinity. This is not the kind of danger that compels people to develop strategies to emasculate you in a way that softens you.

No, I am speaking of danger that truly defines your masculinity. What makes you so dangerous, you might ask? You are dangerous when you are independent. It is not that you don't ever need help, or won't ask for it: you are just not looking for any handouts.

You are dangerous when you can embrace and display emotions. A real man is not afraid to own how he feels. I was raised in the era when men weren't encouraged to display how they felt. You were taught not to cry, even when the pain was more than you could bear. My middle name was "hardness," because that was Survival 101. I spent most of my adult life living along the lines of how I would handle a situation, not how I felt about the situation. My wife would come to me and ask me, "How do you feel about that?" My responses were always some variation on, "Men don't interpret situations based on how they feel, but by what they would do." I was wrong…I was created to have emotions that I don't need to be ashamed of. That's why I mourn, cry, get angry, grieve, laugh, or feel disappointed at times. Those are all emotions that are legitimate, and I embrace them with pride. I believe it was the Wisdom of Solomon that said:

"A time to weep, and a time to laugh; a time to mourn, and a time to dance."—Ecclesiastes 3:4

You are dangerous when you maintain your competitive edge. Every morning you awaken with a plan to make yourself better. There is a strategy for improving your body, soul, and mind.

There is something incredibly unpredictable about a man who is comfortable and confident in who he is. A man in touch with his nature can be intimidating to those who seek to control him and the world around him. In a world that is framed by fear and deception, a man who can persevere and endure with reckless abandon is not easy to predict.

For this reason, the world seeks to alter the route of young boys before they discover their trade secret for success in this world. A systematic formula, to cut the cocoon before the butterfly has come into itself, is producing a culture of men who were robbed of the confidence they would have gained while pressing through adversity in their youth, designed to show them their own strength.

This is what *The Best Man Project* is about: redefining and igniting your passion for who you are, not conforming to what the culture sees or says.

You are wild, adventurous, and dangerous. Now that you know who you are as a man, in the next several chapters I want to show you how this discovery is displayed in your roles as husbands, fathers, and brothers.

REFLECTION PAGE

INTRODUCTION

BEST MAN: Being asked to be the best man in a wedding is a great honor. We aren't bestowed with the title "best" very often in our lives. It shows that your friend or family member holds your relationship in great esteem. You've been his go-to guy in life; now he needs you to be his point person during this weighty rite of passage. So don't just shuffle through your role; instead, help your buddy through the most important day of his life by stepping up and fulfilling your duties with competence. Are you still that *best man*?

DISCUSSION QUESTIONS

1. Talk about what it meant to you when you were asked to be a best man. What are some of the things you did to support the groom-to-be and prepare for your role?

2. What were some of the qualities that you considered when you chose the person who stood by your side at your wedding?

3. In this book, the author implies that "Every man contains the best to be the best, but God is the one to activate that best." How does that statement challenge you to allow God to activate the best in you?

4. Talk about the last time you felt celebrated as a man. How can you escort your son or another man to this celebration?

5. What is the one area in your life that you need to work on and what do you need to work out, as you seek to be the best man God has called you to be? How can the men in your circles support you?

MOVING FORWARD

You are dangerous when you maintain your competitive edge. Every morning you awaken with a plan to make yourself better. There is a strategy for improving your body, soul, and mind.

CHANGING YOUR MIND

This is what The Best Man Project is about: redefining and igniting your passion for who you are, not conforming to what the culture sees or says.

A Man's Prayer

Lord, make me so mighty in my manhood that I defeat every impulse in my soul that seeks to destroy that identity I have in you. Help me to live out my wild, adventurous, and dangerous self with all humility and meekness. May I be granted the grace to balance toughness and tenderness at the same time. Thank you for providing me with positive examples of manhood. Amen!

CHAPTER 8

THE BEST HUSBAND

Now that I know I am a man who has been designed by God to be wild, adventurous, and dangerous, how does that translate into my role as a husband?

At the writing of this book, I have been married nearly three decades. You can't have been married that long and not have something to say on the subject. To be honest, I wouldn't be the husband that I am if it were not for the wife she is. Don't worry, I am not going to bore you with every single detail of our lives over the past thirty years, but the lessons I have learned in my relationship with this incredible woman can serve as a good illustration for you about how to be the best husband.

HE SAID, SHE SAID

The story of how Ingrid and I met comes with its own twists, depending on who is telling it. I first met her while stationed in San Vito, Italy. We were both Air Force service members on our first duty assignment after military school. I arrived a couple months before her. One of the requirements that had to be met by all those first assigned to the base was to pick your chemical warfare gear. My pastor and I were taking a walk when we came up on her, lugging her gear to the dorm room. We asked if she needed any assistance, and I proceeded to grab the bag and walk it up to her room. Now, she tells the story that there is no memory of me carrying the gear for her.

But we both agree that our next encounter happened when we were working the same shift and I asked her if she wanted to attend a Bible Study afterwards. She initially said no, to which I sarcastically said, "I do not want to sleep with you." She would later change her mind and accept the invitation. Later she made the decision to connect to God, and was baptized in the Adriatic Sea. She asked me to attend this incredible moment in her life.

We decided to teach a kids' class together, and eventually became the best of friends. To let her tell it, she was not the least bit interested in me romantically; that was fine by me, because I had my eyes on the prize.

My proposal for marriage came out of nowhere. We were having a simple dinner and out of my mouth blurted, "Will you marry me?" The rest, as they say, is history!

But one thing that she never knew prior to that moment, long before our paths crossed, I stood out on the steps of my dorm one starry night and prayed, asking God to send me a wife. I know that sounds corny, but it really did happen. Let's just say that I am more than grateful that I had a little heavenly help with finding her.

WIRED FOR PARTNERSHIP

It is not good for men to be alone. We are wired for partnership. In Genesis 2:15, God made His instructions clear to Adam. He put Adam in the garden and assigned him to take care of it. Then God gave him permission to enjoy the fruit of the garden, with the exception of the tree of knowledge of good and evil. All of this, before he even had a mate.

There is no doubt that because Adam knew who he was as a man that this would help prepare him for his role as a husband. Here are God's own words to Adam:

"It isn't good for the man to live alone. I need to make a suitable partner for him."—Genesis 2:18 (CEV)

When did the suitable partner come for him? After Adam knew about work and following instructions. Plus, you add a wild side, adventure, and a little danger, and you have a modern day James Bond or Jason Bourne.

God's definition of manhood is the ability to take those innate traits and put them into action at home with your wife and family. No amount of strength, good looks, or money can upgrade your actions when it comes to being a man with your wife.

We have a tendency to adapt to the cultural standards when it comes to our identity. We base that identity on clothes, shoes, cars, and female conquests. But that directs us to a primitive nature that we were not designed for.

How many athletic jerseys do you have that have another man's name on them? I catch the best pass through Dez Bryant; run my fastest through Usain Bolt; hit the best 3-pointer through Steph Curry; shoot the lowest score through Phil Mickelson. There is a danger in living out our lives not in our own names.

My wife didn't marry me for what I had. She married me for who I was and who she had hoped I would become in the future. We are partners in this marriage. My wife has a saying that she reminds me of often: "You are the hamburger and I am your hamburger helper."

MY RESPONSIBILITY

If I have learned anything over these years, it is that I am responsible for how I function in my marriage. I can't point fingers or pass the blame to anyone when it comes to how I relate to Ingrid. I used to think that I could blame it on my upbringing, cultural moorings, or a lack of knowledge, but in reality I have had to own my stuff.

As a man, I assume the part I play in providing the safety and security needs of a wife who relies on our family direction and destiny.

My spiritual father Larry Titus would teach me another major responsibility of mine in my marriage, and that is knowing the difference between headship and leadership. I am the head in my house, but I don't lead in all things in my house. He would go on to teach that headship and leadership are not synonymous. Headship in a marriage is a gender issue, and leadership is a personality trait.

Let me make it clear, headship is not a right to be earned, but a responsibility given. This God-given role is not assigned to you as a man because you are better, faster, or stronger. And no, it is not because you are better looking, either. So, don't exert a spirit of superiority in your marriage as though you are the more right between you. This is not a superior or inferior dynamic. Headship is about providing the primary direction for the home.

Now, when it comes to leadership in the relationship, a man recognizes he cannot do everything in a marriage. There will be some things you will make the best leader for, but there may very well be a whole lot of things that your wife can lead in. If you are not good at managing money, give the lead to your wife. If you are better at cooking, then you take the lead. I have met a number of men who are outstanding cooks and do all the cooking in the home.

The most important thing that I have learned over the years is that releasing my wife to lead in those areas she is most gifted in not only demonstrates the greatest act of selflessness for me, it frees us to have balance in our marriage. Having a shared load bearing was freeing for the both us.

Let me say one more thing about responsibility that provided an underlining foundation for me. Marriage was

God's idea, and He laid the responsibility for the home squarely on the man. Just ask Adam in the Bible. Even though it was Eve who plucked the forbidden fruit and gave it to her husband, God came looking for Adam. And when Adam tried to point the finger at Eve, God would not take the bait. A man who has allowed his manhood to be shaped by our Creator will step up and fill the role of a husband without an inferiority complex, but a God-designed complex.

WIFE LEARNING 101

A man never stops learning. Whether it is reading books, mastering a hobby, or knowing about legislation that shapes your community, you can't educate yourself too much. But there is no better course for every husband to take - Wife Learning 101.

My wife Ingrid is beautiful, intelligent, and wonderfully witty. She often tells people that when we awaken in the morning the first question I generally ask her is, "Who are you today?" Every day is a lesson with her. I get to learn how valuable a treasure she is and how incredibly lucky I am, which made me realize how huge my responsibility is to love and honor her God's way.

Speaking of which, I have learned a lot about the heart of God through her. I have told her often how she models the spirit of generosity and the gift of hospitality toward strangers for me. I have had repeated reminders that God does not just talk to me, but can deliver heart-shaping, destiny-shifting instruction through my wife (and my children, too).

Don't be afraid to dig in and make the commitment to know her through every season of her life. Get to know her emotions, moods, and joys, so you will know how to respond and not react. This learning concept for me was driven home by a passage out of the Bible.

In 1 Peter 3:7, the apostle gives husbands some very important insight into their wives and how to treat them.

"Husbands, in the same way be considerate as you live with your wives, and treat them with respect as the weaker partner and as heirs with you of the gracious gift of life, so that nothing will hinder your prayers."

Peter is advising in that verse that we are to be understanding to the woman that we married. He is saying that we need to study them. Study the Word and study your wife; you will not go wrong. I am not going to sugarcoat, it, but both are difficult to learn. Yet the amount of treasure you discover richly pays off in the long run.

Peter also goes on to say that we are to treat our wives with respect. I believe that means encouraging, pampering, and loving her in the same way you did when you were courting her. Dating your wife does not end when you say, "I do."

One reason we are to live with our wives in a loving and sacrificial way is so that nothing will hinder our prayers. If you are determined not to love her unconditionally, take the licks of the world for her, or if you are not going to learn about her, then don't get down to pray.

SILENT TREATMENT

A married couple had a quarrel, and ended up giving each other the silent treatment. Two days into their mute argument, the man realized he needed his wife's help. In order to catch a flight to Chicago for a business meeting, he had to get up at 5 a.m.

Not wanting to be the first to break the silence, he wrote on a piece of paper, "Please wake me at 5 a.m."

The next morning the man woke up only to discover his wife was already out of bed. It was 9 a.m., and his flight had long since departed. He was about to find his wife and demand an answer for her failings when he noticed a piece of paper by the bed. He read, "It's 5 a.m. Wake up."

There is a lot of silent treatment in marriages because of what is brought to the marriage. Many areas are left undiscovered and unexplored because of family, social, and cultural constructs.

If there is one thing I have learned over the years, it is that *communication is crucial.* The saying around our home is, "The lack of communication will lead to speculation."

From one brother to another, I challenge you to practice keeping the lines of communication open with your wife. Be proactive and open about discussing anything. Talking things out, no matter how uncomfortable it may be, will be your greatest triumph. Don't shut down, even when you hit a roadblock.

Love unconditionally, forgive quickly, esteem her higher than yourself, sacrifice for her until it hurts, hold her hand in public, speak her love language—and if all else fails, try again. If you do this, God will blossom and develop her into a woman of grace and true beauty. Then you will be truly satisfied. I love you, Ingrid!

REFLECTION PAGE

INTRODUCTION

BEST HUSBAND: Marriage is hard, and often we encounter problems we just did not expect and have no idea how to deal with. *Why did she say that? Why is she upset about this? Is having sex____ times a week normal?* As we learn how to be married, and as we continue to encounter new stages in life (through the newlywed period, moves, jobs, becoming parents, parenting teens, etc.), it is extremely helpful to discover what being a husband is all about, and be the best you can be at it. Are you still that *best husband*?

DISCUSSION QUESTIONS

1. Talk about how you were raised, and its effect on the way you see yourself as a husband. What are some of things you learned, or did not learn, from other married men in your family?

2. Knowing what you know now, would you have waited before getting married? Describe the kind of sitcom/movie husband you most identify with.

3. In this chapter, the author would like to suggest that, "Finding another husband who has been down your road before and lived to tell the tale is worth his weight in gold." How does that statement challenge you to find a husband mentor?

4. Talk about the last time you felt honored as a husband by your wife. When was the last time you gave honor to your wife? What needs to be reviewed and renewed between the two of you?

5. What is the one area in your life as a husband (or potential husband) that you need to work on? How can the men in your circles support you?

MOVING FORWARD

My question for us all today is: how will your marriage be different going forward? How is it going to get better? How can you be a better husband? Has there been a growing distance between you and your wife? How can you become close again? We must be intentional about our marriages, or they're going to die of neglect. Will you find your mentor?

CHANGING YOUR MIND

"For the husband is the head of the wife as Christ is the head of the church"—Eph. 5:23

A MAN'S PRAYER

God, thank You for my wife. She is a gift from You. Help me to be quick to forgive, ready to encourage, and always available to her. Give me guidance as I seek to meet her needs and be her leader. Help me be faithful to her in my mind, thoughts, and heart. Keep us focused on You as we go through trials and times of conflict. Help us to work out conflict in a way that honors You. I commit my marriage to You. AMEN!

CHAPTER 9

THE BEST FATHER

George Lucas, the creator of *Star Wars*, was being interviewed by television journalist Charlie Rose. The interview went on for about an hour, about his role as a writer, director, film producer, and technology innovator. They discussed the success of the *Star Wars* franchise and all of the other major accomplishments he'd made in his life.

Charlie ended the interview with this profound question: "When you die, what would you like the first line of your obituary to read?"

George Lucas replied, "That I was a good dad."

That's a powerful statement. Out of all of his accomplishments and what he did to help change the film industry, his role as a father is the one he most wants to be remembered for. Something that is lost on fatherhood in America today for those who do not take it seriously.

I am a proud father of four children, three sons and one daughter. They have made me so proud of what they have become and what they are becoming; the honor is all mine, to be their Dad. Each one of them has their own unique qualities, passions, and drives. I know their likes, many of their habits, and most of their dislikes. Each one has pulled the best out of me.

When you have multiple children, it becomes difficult at times to treat them as individuals, while at the same time keeping the family together as one unit. So, what I would do for them when they were younger was schedule each their own special day. It would be a day when we spent exclusively one-on-one time. We didn't have to share the time with their other siblings, because they too would have their special day.

What I learned during those moments, while being a part of my children's lives and raising them, was that my role *was a whole lot more important than I would ever imagine.*

I have come to understand over the course of time that a boy learns how to treat a woman by the way he sees his father treat his mother. And a daughter determines and decides relationships with men by the relationship she has with her father. So, you can see the hard journey it creates for them, if the father is absent.

A BIBLE LESSON

Throughout the Old Testament and even in some chapters in the New Testament, you find the son always connected to his father. I believe it provided for a most important identity marking. Matthew 1:1–3 reads:

> *"This is the genealogy of Jesus the Messiah the son of David, the son of Abraham: Abraham was the father of Isaac, Isaac the father of Jacob, Jacob the father of Judah and his brothers, Judah the father of Perez and Zerah, whose mother was Tamar, Perez the father of Hezron, Hezron the father of Ram..."*

Jesus himself would identify Himself as a son and God as His father.

"Don't you believe that I am in the Father, and that the Father is in me? The words I say to you I do not speak on my own authority. Rather, it is the Father, living in me, who is doing his work."—John 14:10

When you read the Bible, you will find a clear division between the Old Testament and the New Testament. The last Old Testament book is Malachi. I want to answer the question as to what are the final words of this final book, before you read the first words of the New Testament book Matthew.

"Behold, I will send you Elijah the prophet before the coming of the great and dreadful day of the LORD. And he will turn the hearts of the fathers to the children, and the hearts of the children to their fathers,"—Malachi 4:5–6

I pray that Elijah the prophet comes quickly!

IT TAKES A MAN TO RAISE A MAN

The first time a man wrestled with his identity was as a little boy. While it is understandable that a girl doesn't need to fall down and get dirty, that is not true for a boy. A boy needs to fall, because it's not how many blows he can take, it is how many times he can get back up. In getting back up from a blow, a boy draws strength and over time develops a natural resistance to and tolerance for pain. It is this resistance that will be revisited as a man as he seeks to secure his manhood. When a boy is allowed room to fall, he is allowed room to grow.

If she isn't careful, a mother may unknowingly cause the son to miscarry critical traits he will need in adulthood only to find they are not available to him. A boy needs a father to give him wisdom on every matter because he needs that male perspective.

A father can model exactly how a boy's life should be balanced. "There is a time to cry and a time not to cry," is an old proverb. But a father would be the example, showing his son how a man can know when. He will know when his son needs a hug, and when his son needs to stand alone and figure things out on his own.

When the family dynamic is broken down, the wife or mother is left to lead her son down a path of manhood that she has never traveled herself.

Men may play a vital role in how the world is shaped, but their role in the lives of their sons is the most critical.

Unfortunately, if there is not a man in the home operating in this role, it can be difficult for a young boy to know what kind of man he is. Not all men are the same, and it is important to understand how we are different so that we are secure in functioning as a little boy, young adult, and eventually, a grown man (rite of passage, if you will).

Women who are forced to raise their sons alone are most commended. A noble task to assume, but in all honesty, one that can take her away from her natural element, which would cause imbalance in her own life. I've heard many say they are both the mother and father to their children.

While that coined phrase is trending worldwide, and is usually received with a standing ovation, it is against nature and it is not possible. A woman can never teach a boy how to transition to manhood, because she has never gone through it herself.

There are so many mothers who seek to fix the failures of men, who don't stay and raise the children they sire, by teaching their sons to be the men who never go away. I have witnessed mothers encouraging their daughters to go out and conquer the world, only to discourage their sons from ever successfully disconnecting from the invisible umbilical cord.

In the end, the boy suffers from an identity crisis. Instead of being who he's supposed to be, he becomes the man the mother never wants to leave her. Instead of being who he's supposed to be, he becomes her *provider;* she sends him off to work or professional athletics, so he can become rich and buy her a house to pay her back for all she's done for him as a single mom, and make up the difference for the man who didn't come and sweep her off her feet as a knight in shining armor. Instead of being who he's supposed to be, he becomes her *security blanket* and she allows him to live in her home rent free, along with his girlfriend and children, and all of his friends make her house the place to be.

If you are a single mother reading this section, I mean no offense. I just want to make sure I am clear. A boy needs his mother, but as the boy comes of age he will need his father more. Don't allow any disagreements that you may have with the father to disconnect him from his son.

Now, I know you want to ask, "What if the father is not in his life?" Then, I suggest that you connect him with a man in the family, such as grandfather, brother, or uncle. Or connect to a local church that offers a mentor program for young boys. Also, the Big Brothers/Big Sisters is a great mentoring program.

A DAUGHTER NEEDS HER DAD

I believe that there are tons of fathers out there who melt at the phrase, "Daddy's girl." It gets to me every time I hear it ringing in my ears. It just melts my heart into pieces. It has a way of softening me up when I think I am being the hardest toward this young woman, my daughter, whom we named Charis.

I remember the day my wife came home from a conference in Arizona. She was instructed with some of the other ladies in attendance to get away, so that they might hear from God. She told me that when she got to that quiet place with Him, it was revealed to her that we were to have another child.

Now mind you, it had been nearly four years since we'd had our last child and we didn't have any plans for any more. But when God says yes, who were we to say no? Even her name was a directive. Charis means God's gift of grace. And every time we call her name, we are reminded of God's graciousness toward us. I would be lying to you if I said she didn't have me wrapped around her little finger.

She has shown me so much and tempered me in ways that I never could have imagined. But I am constantly aware that she excels in beauty, brains, and boldness. I know that my relationship with her produces character that prepares her for the world she enters into every day.

As a father, this is what I have learned that a daughter needs in her life:

VISIBLE PRESENCE

There is nothing more important than a dad being present in the life of his daughter. I mean really being present. Listening to her, supporting her, and encouraging her shapes what she feels about herself, and provides steady guidance. It gives her a strong sense of security.

One of the things I did with my daughter, when she was very young, was to be her very first date. I went through this whole formality of asking her mom, *"May I take her out?"* I made a reservation at a restaurant, got the car washed. At 4 o'clock I stepped outside, knocked on the door, escorted my daughter to the car, opened the door, drove to the restaurant, ordered the meal for her, paid for the meal, brought her home at a decent hour (it was 6 o'clock, since she was only 4 years of age at the time). I wanted her to know that whenever she went out on a date (that's if she ever goes out on a date—I am a pit-bull) that is how she should be treated. I have been escorting her ever since.

UNCONDITIONAL LOVE

More than anything else, a daughter needs unconditional love from her father. Love covers a multitude of fears, sins, and mistakes. Daughters will not be hungry for male love in an atmosphere where she is loved unconditionally.

A REAL HERO

A daughter needs a father to respect. She will never know about boundaries or have respect for your directions if she does not respect you. Intimidation as a practice will lead to rebellion when she is a teenager. You want your daughter to grow up following your lead because she loves you and honors you. She needs a hero that is strong and tender at the same time.

Things like speaking truth, offering encouragement, and being transparent puts you in place ahead of any man that she will ever encounter in her life. In fact, you will be the go-to model for all time. Put away your cape, and just take her out for ice cream and show her some love.

I also recommend a great movie that you two can watch together, that really illustrates that bond she needs with you. Our favorite is the movie *Taken*, starring Liam Neeson. It is a movie about the lengths a father will go to, to protect and rescue his daughter. We love that movie because it displays a father's love for his daughter at the highest level.

YOU ARE THE MAN FOR THE JOB

Listen, your son needs you and your daughter needs you. This is not the time to disappear and take off from fatherhood. Fathers, you are the man for the job. You have developed a certain set of skills that will impact your family for a lifetime.

I'll leave you with this verse to ponder from Ephesians 6:4.

"Fathers, don't make your children bitter about life. Instead, bring them up in Christian discipline and instruction."

Reflection Page

INTRODUCTION

BEST FATHER: Men may play a vital role in how the world is shaped, but their role in the lives of their sons is the most critical. Unfortunately, if there is not a man in the home operating in this role, it can be difficult for a young boy to know what kind of man he is. Will you step up to the plate and be the best father?

DISCUSSION QUESTIONS

1. Think about the role your father did or did not play in your life growing up. What are points of struggle for you?

2. Knowing that it takes a man to raise a man, describe the ways that you are currently active in your own son's life. What areas do you think you can step up in?

3. In this chapter, the author stated, "Men play a vital role in the lives of their sons." How does that statement challenge you to become more actively involved in shaping your son's life?

4. Talk about the last time you lifted up your daughter's self-esteem. Are you ready to take strides in unconditional love toward her, and show her heroism?

5. What is one area in your life as a father or potential father that you need to work on? How can your brothers support you?

MOVING FORWARD

I know that it is not easy fathering in the times that we live in, but if not you, then who? No one can have as much influence and impact on your children, grandchildren, nephews, nieces, and the like. So it's time that you move forward, not worrying about what you may not have gotten from your father. You are going to do great!

CHANGING YOUR MIND

"Fathers, do not exasperate your children; instead, bring them up in the training and instruction of the Lord."—Eph. 6:4

A Man's Prayer

Creator God, thank You for creating me to share in the conception of life, and share in the responsibility of raising my children. I ask that You would help me as I train up my children to know You and love You. As I look to You as my Father, may I give Your love to my children. God, give me the compassion and tenderness my children need. Give me courage and strength to live according to Your guidance and wisdom. Help me correct them when needed and encourage them always. Amen!

CHAPTER 10

THE BEST BROTHER

I am a task-oriented and goal-setting person. This is usually how I operate, and there is a lot that gets accomplished in my life. Now there's nothing wrong with setting goals and forging ahead to complete them, but often I have done it at the expense of building relationships along the way.

I will be the first one to raise my hand to say loudly that I had my share of Lone Ranger moments. There has been a saturation of independence in my veins. I wore the mask and played the role. Some of that comes from being both stung and stabbed before. Once you've been stabbed, you don't want to go through that again. So, a self-reliant focus is what I developed over the years.

Now, I'm getting better. I'm not where I want to be yet, but at least I'm not where I was. God has connected me with some very important men in my life, to help me to learn how to work the journey of establishing authentic—not just casual—acquaintances.

This no doubt describes a lot of you reading this chapter. You pride yourself on being a loner. You don't need anyone to do anything for you. You have your game face on and your head down, as you move toward advancements, promotions, and career objectives.

Yet we men very rarely stop and take time for authentic relationships, because we believe they are just a necessary evil. But you can never work through this manhood crisis without meaningful relationships in your life. You were not meant to be alone (read Genesis 2:18), and that doesn't just apply to having a wife.

AM I MY BROTHER'S KEEPER?

Many of us are most familiar with the story of Cain and Abel; it's one of the most recounted and frequently depicted Bible stories. Cain is jealous of his brother, and seriously angry with God. God offers him a way to squash the envious feeling that he was carrying in his heart toward his brother.

But Genesis 4:8 reads:

"Now Cain said to his brother Abel, 'Let's go out to the field.' While they were in the field, Cain attacked his brother Abel and killed him."

Cain lured his brother out into a field and killed him. I pray that we are not leading our brothers out into fields and taking their lives. But are we? I grieve every time I hear the news of a man taking the life of another man.

That's another man who doesn't get a chance to grow old with his wife; another man who does not get to raise his children, into adulthood and beyond; another man who will not be a vital source of modeling and mentoring in our communities.

But the next exchange between God and Cain will be replayed throughout history.

"Then the LORD said to Cain, 'Where is your brother Abel?' 'I don't know,' he replied. 'Am I my brother's keeper?'"— Genesis 4:9

It's as if God is interrogating us with the same question, "Where is your brother?" You know someone has been missing from the front lines of leading their family. There are men in your inner circles who have been missing in action from Church and community.

But we have become so used to being alone that overlooking the mass casualties of men left on the battlefield of life is too common. Being an Air Force veteran, I was always taught never to leave a man behind.

We have operated alone for so long, being largely unaware of our brother's presence and plight. When we are asked where is our brother, our only answer is, "I don't know."

DEACTIVATION

I recently received a notification from the bank advising me that someone fraudulently gaining my debit card information compromised my privacy information. As a result, a third-party source gained access to my personal information. While identity theft has long been an issue in our society, we are actively living in the most dangerous day and time for counterfeit information, with the advances of digital technology.

In an effort to protect its interest and my faith and trust in its institution, the bank deactivated my account and replaced the old information with a new, encrypted debit card.

I believe God has been speaking to each of our hearts to let us know that there has been a breach of data. His original purpose for man has been intercepted and hijacked, and this independent spirit is having unparalleled effects on families, culture, and race.

The challenge for men is that we have to get the word out to all men that access to the new image and likeness of God is available for activation through Jesus Christ, and that we need to walk this out together.

But, we must deactivate the thought that all men are dogs and predators on the prowl, seeking whomever we will devour next. We need to separate ourselves from those who have convinced us that femininity is acceptable and masculinity is intimidating. We must deconstruct the myths produced by a few who left legacies of destruction. We must tear down the walls that separate us, and re-establish manhood.

We need to deactivate old paradigm shifts concerning manhood and masculinity. We are not monsters; we are men.

We are not moronic; we are men. We are not misfits; we are men. We may be messy at times, but we are still men.

REACTIVATION

Acquaintances are nice to have, but relationships are essential for us to finish strong. We need men in our lives. Look at what Paul tells us:

"Brothers, if someone is caught in a sin, you who are spiritual should restore him gently... Carry each other's burdens, and in this way you will fulfill the law of Christ."—Galatians 6:1–2

You and I can't restore any man if we are not close enough to know that he is hurting, or that he would be comfortable admitting he needs help.

We need to reactivate some tools to help us reconnect and be able to answer the question of *am I my brother's keeper* with a resounding yes!

I sense that this activation begins with recognizing that every man needs three kinds of friends in his life.

1. A PAUL

This is an older, mature man in your life, a father figure. This person would be someone who has been where we are trying to go. This is where you swallow your pride and start asking questions about life and how to navigate it. Some of you would need a spiritual father in your life right about now. You should pray to ask God to open your heart, and allow a Paul-type figure to come into your life. You have some major decisions to make, and you'll need the wisdom of a godly man to provide it.

2. A BARNABAS

This man is like a brother. Somebody who loves you, but is not impressed with what you have or where you have been. This is the one who represents your equal and can relate to you on that level. He is your sounding board, and your accountability partner. Barnabas' name means "son of comfort." He would encourage you, and you would encourage him.

3. A TIMOTHY

So, you have a father and a brother; you will also need a son. There are a lot of young men and boys out there who do not have a father or father figure in their life. That is where you come along. They need someone to look up to, someone to model what a man is supposed to look like.

If you want to know what this look likes, take a look at all the sports teams where there are young men and boys being coached every day. You know what we call this—mentoring. And without you knowing it, some younger man is watching you for ideas on how to do a job, talk to a woman, express himself in a respectful manner, or he's simply wanting to know how to tie that necktie.

THE BEST MAN PROJECT

That is why this project is so important to me. This is about starting a movement, not just a moment. This book may not be long in chapters, but I hope it is long on substance. I want to make a difference, first by being a man and then continuing to work it into my roles as husband and father.

I invite you to do the same, but let's go one further; let's intentionally make friends along the way. There is no way we are going to be able to do this alone. Someone once said, "If you are not dead, God's not done with you."

Last time I checked, the train has not pulled out from the station yet. You still have time to get a ticket and get on board.

I know you may feel like you have a lot a baggage filled with failures, mistakes, and missteps. You may arrive at the station with family faults, personal regrets, and spiritual setbacks.

There is something you should know about God—He has grace. If you make a commitment to Christ, you'll find that everything will take care of itself.

I want to leave you with this word: I am determined not to leave any man behind. I will continue to be in relentless pursuit of my sons. I will text, tweet, and talk to the men in my life. I am ready to make new connections and help to raise the flag at the top of the hill, with these words inscribed on it—I AM A MAN!

REFLECTION PAGE

INTRODUCTION

BEST BROTHER: There is a Bible verse that tells us that iron sharpens iron, and so does the countenance of another man. It generally doesn't take women long to click and forge relationships that last a lifetime. But for men, it is a task that proves to be a lot more difficult. We form a general practice of choosing paths of loneliness, and wear them like badges of honor. But we cannot go it alone. Are you your brother's keeper?

DISCUSSION QUESTIONS

1. Talk about your memories of the childhood friend, college brother, or work colleague that has greatly impacted your life. Do you remember what connected you to him?

2. Is there a tendency for you to do things alone? Is it a challenge for you to connect with other men? Why or why not? Have you ever reached out first to form authentic relationships?

3. In this chapter, the author stated that relationships are essential. We need other men in our lives. How do you feel about that statement? Is it easy or hard to admit?

4. Talk about the time when a brother came to bail you out of a situation you got stuck in. Did that encourage you as a man? Share a time when you were there for a brother. How did it strengthen him?

5. What is one area in your life as a brother that you need to work on? How can other brothers support you?

MOVING FORWARD

The days of men going it alone are fading fast. Men are recognizing that there is need for accountability and activity among men. We were not designed to go it alone. Let's turn the page and forge a new chapter in relationship building. Yes, women have a head start, but that doesn't mean we can't catch up.

CHANGING YOUR MIND

"As iron sharpens iron, so one man sharpens another."—Proverbs 27:17

A Man's Prayer

Lord, make my life like a trunk and branches so mightily tough and impervious to wind and drought that I never cease to engage in developing healthy relationships with other men. Help me to know that You did not create man to be alone and that I can't walk this journey on my own. Help me to learn how to forge new relationships that will keep me accountable in the days to come. Amen!

EPILOGUE

I'm a big fan of the movie *300*, with Gerald Butler as Leonidas, King of Sparta. The plot revolves around King Leonidas (Gerard Butler), who leads 300 Spartans into battle against the Persian god-king Xerxes (Rodrigo Santoro) and his invading army of more than 300,000 soldiers.

Leonidas repeatedly makes impassioned speeches about the values Sparta holds dear. These include glory, reason, justice, respect, family and freedom. *Bravery* is hardly a strong enough word to describe these warriors' fearlessness. Dying on Sparta's behalf is the highest possible honor.

Spartan war tactics depend on interdependence. Leonidas says, "A Spartan's strength is the warrior next to him." The king's willingness to sacrifice himself for his men contrasts with Xerxes' megalomania; the Persian ruler willingly sends hundreds to their deaths, with no concern for their welfare. The only men Leonidas invites to join his war party are those with sons, lest any family's line be wiped out.

One scene in the movie stood out to me in particular. It was when Leonidas encounters Ephialtes, a deformed Spartan whose parents fled Sparta to spare him certain infanticide. Ephialtes asks to redeem his father's name by joining Leonidas' army, warning him of a secret (goat) path the Persians could use to outflank and surround the Spartans.

Though sympathetic, Leonidas rejects him since his deformity physically prevents him from properly holding his shield; this could compromise the phalanx formation. This weakness would leave the men vulnerable.

What men need to understand today is that we are in a war for our manhood and our masculinity. Our victory depends on the man standing next to us. What men need to hear today is: "You don't have to make any excuses for warrior strength."

Most of all, men need to know that real men can be tough and tender, rugged and romantic, strong and soothing at the same time.

Men need to know that we are stronger through interdependence than independence. You cannot stand alone facing the challenge of keeping your family ahead of your career. You cannot stand alone raising kids who are not directionless, but destined. You cannot stand alone when it comes to honoring women rather than ogling them. You cannot stand alone when it comes to impacting your community and your culture.

Men need to know that gaining more power, filling more prisons, and generating more children out of wedlock doesn't define our manhood.

Men need to know that leaving charity to the government and church to the girls are not the marks of manhood, but trails of boyhood tolerated.

And finally, men need to know that the man standing next to you is facing the same fight, the same obstacles, and the same road; together we will be able to tell our sons the same words King David said to Solomon, "Be a man."

Together we can be redeemers, restorers, and a reflection of strong passionate men who know that we don't check out, we check in.

Brothers, I ask you, will you be my *best man*?

Made in the USA
Middletown, DE
23 February 2016